Dog Books: 101 Amazing Facts about Dogs

Dog Books for Kids

Learn More about Man's Best Friend

Jenny Kellett

ISBN-13: 978-1530322145
ISBN-10: 1530322146

World's Best Facts
www.worldsbestfacts.com
Email: me@jennykellett.com

Printed in U.S.A

Introduction

It's hard not to love dogs, in fact 1 in 3 American families have at least one pooch! But how much do you know about your puppy or dog?

In this book you will learn over 100 amazing new things about your best friend. From the huge Great Dane's to the tiny Chihuahua, you'll be a cynologist (an expert in dogs) in no time!

Are you ready? Let's go!

Dog Facts

Dogs are mentioned 14 times in the Bible.

• • • • •

City dogs live three years longer than a country dog, on average.

• • • • •

Dalmatians are born completely white.

• • • • •

In 1957, a dog named Laika was launched into space on the Russian spacecraft Sputnik 2.

Kelpie puppy.

Dogs don't like the rain because the sound is too loud for their ears.

• • • • •

Border Collies and Poodles are considered to be the smartest dog breeds, whereas Afghan hounds and the Basenji are the least intelligent.

• • • • •

The oldest dog on record was an Australian Cattle Dog called Bluey who lived until he was 29 years old.

• • • • •

The Taco Bell Chihuahua is a rescued dog named Gidget.

Old English Sheepdog.

In seven years, one female dog and her female children could produce 4,372 puppies!

• • • • •

Dogs only have sweat glands in between their paw pads - no where else.

Some studies have shown that dogs can detect cancer by smelling a person's breath.

• • • • •

Greyhounds can run up to 45 miles an hour!

• • • • •

The real name of Toto the dog in the movie Wizard of Oz was Terry.

• • • • •

The smallest dog on record was a Yorkshire Terrier from Great Britain who, at the age of two, weighed just four ounces.

• • • • •

If you spay/neuter your dog before it turns six months old, you can lower its risk of getting cancer.

• • • • •

Female dogs carry their puppies for about 60 days before they are born.

• • • • •

Davy Crockett had a dog named Sport.

• • • • •

A dog's level of intelligence is equivalent to that of a human two year old.

• • • • •

A dog's heart beat is between 70 and 120 pulses a minute. A human's heart beats between 70 and 80 times a minute.

• • • • •

The most popular names for a male dog are Max and Jake. The most popular female names are Maggie and Molly.

• • • • •

The highest dog population in the world is in the USA. France comes second.

• • • • •

A dog's sense of smell is 100,000 times stronger than that of humans.

A dog's ear has over 18 muscles in it.

• • • • •

Dogs were the first animals domesticated by humans.

• • • • •

The shape of a dog's face can help predict how long it will live.

• • • • •

A dog's nose has over 200 scent-receiving cells.

• • • • •

George Washington had 36 dogs — all foxhounds.

Beagle.

Every year, 15 people in the USA die from dog bites.

• • • • •

There are different smells in a dog's urine, which tells other dogs whether that dog is male or female, old or young, and sick or healthy.

• • • • •

Just like human babies, Chihuahua puppies are born with a soft spot in their skull which closes up with age.

• • • • •

Even just small quantities of grapes, raisins and chocolates can cause serious illness for your dog.

Bulldog.

Rottweiler puppy.

People who own pets are said to live longer, have less stress and have fewer heart attacks.

• • • • •

Dog nose prints are as unique as human fingerprints and can be used to identify them.

• • • • •

Studies show that petting a dog can lower your blood pressure.

• • • • •

Apple and pear seeds contain a chemical called arsenic, which can be deadly to dogs.

More than 1 in 3 American families own a dog.

• • • • •

Greyhounds have the best eyesight of any breed of dog.

• • • • •

Adult dogs have 42 teeth.

• • • • •

80 per cent of dog owners give their dogs gifts on holidays such as Christmas and birthdays.

• • • • •

Dogs' shoulder blades are not attached to their skeletons, allowing them to run.

Border Collie.

The first sense puppies develop is touch.

• • • • •

Dogs have twice as many muscles in their ears than humans.

• • • • •

Lundehund dogs have six toes on each foot!

• • • • •

Despite what many people think, dogs are not colorblind. However, they don't see colors as vividly as humans.

• • • • •

Prairie Dogs actually belong to the squirrel family.

Dalmation.

Just like humans can save lives by donating blood, dogs can do the same! If they share the same blood type, a dogs blood can be used to save another one.

• • • • •

Dogs can understand up to 250 words and gestures and can do basic mathematical calculations.

• • • • •

Some stray dogs in Russia have worked out how to use the subway system to help them get around and find food.

• • • • •

French Bulldog puppy.

Husky.

The Beatles song 'A day in the life' was recorded with a high-pitched whistle playing in the background that only dogs can hear!
Seeing Eye dogs pee and poo on demand, so that their owners know when to clean up after them.

• • • • •

Hyenas are more closely related to cats than dogs.

• • • • •

Spiked dog collars were invented in Ancient Greece to protect dogs from wolf attacks.

• • • • •

Dogs drink water by forming the back of their tongues into a mini cup.

In the USA, over 1 million dog owners have put their dog as the main beneficiary of their will!

• • • • •

Dogs have three eyelids.

• • • • •

The Basenji is the world's only dog that doesn't bark.

• • • • •

There are an estimated 400 million dogs in the world.

Golden Retriever.

33 per cent of dog owners have admitted to talking to their dogs on the phone, some even leave them voicemails!

• • • • •

There are hundreds of different breeds of dog, which are divided into eight different classes: sporting, hound, terrier, working, herding, non-sporting and miscellaneous.

• • • • •

All dogs are descendants of wolves.

• • • • •

Two dogs survived the sinking of the Titanic — a Pomeranian and a Pekingese.

Yorkshire Terrier.

45 per cent of dogs sleep in their owners bed!

• • • • •

Dogs curl up in a ball when they sleep to keep themselves warm and protect themselves from predators.

While Chow Chow dogs are famous for their blue-black tongues, they are actually born with pink tongues. Their tongues change color when they are around 8-10 weeks old.

• • • • •

Puppies get their full set of permanent teeth between four and six months old.

• • • • •

Boxer.

Dogs don't have an appendix.

• • • • •

Despite what many people think, the Canary Islands (a group of islands off the east coast of Africa) weren't named after birds, they were named after the large dogs that lived on the islands.
Domestic dogs are omnivores. This means they eat meat, grains and vegetables.

• • • • •

Dogs bark for a large number of reasons, but often do so to get attention from other people or other dogs. Some other reasons that dogs bark include: to protect their territory, express a need or to initiate play.

Dogs ears move independently of one another.

• • • • •

In their first few weeks of life, puppies spend 90 per cent of each day sleeping.
Chihuahuas were named after the state in Mexico where they were discovered.

• • • • •

The Irish Wolfhound is the world's tallest breed of dog.

• • • • •

4 out of 5 dogs over the age of 3 have gum disease.

• • • • •

A Beagle and a West Highland Terrier.

Dogs can smell when you are sick.

• • • • •

When you smile at your dog with your teeth showing, they don't see it as a smile - they see it as a sign of aggression.

President Lyndon Johnson had two dogs named 'Him' and 'Her'.

• • • • •

Basset Hounds cannot swim.

• • • • •

The St Bernard is, on average, the heaviest dog breed.

• • • • •

There are 6.2 million puppies born each year in the USA. In comparison, only 4 million human babies are born each year.

When a puppy turns one year old it is an adult. In human years, this is around 15 years old.

• • • • •

Puppies start off with 28 teeth before they get their full adult set of 42.

• • • • •

Dogs have a special membrane in their eyes that allows them to see in the dark.

• • • • •

Dogs pant to cool themselves off.

• • • • •

Golden Labradors.

Yorkshire Terrier.

When dogs kick after going to the toilet, it is to spread their scent as far as possible.

• • • • •

Based on the average life span of 11 years, the cost of owning a dog is around $13,500.

• • • • •

A dog's whiskers are touch-sensitive hairs called vibrissae. They are found on the muzzle, above the eyes and below the jaws, and can actually sense tiny changes in airflow.

• • • • •

Smaller breeds of dog mature faster than larger breeds.

• • • • •

Dogs with deep wrinkles need to be washed daily. Dirt can build up leading to odor or infection.

• • • • •

Dogs often react differently to human males and females.

• • • • •

Some dogs lick their paws and then rub their paws on their head to clean themselves, much like a cat!

• • • • •

Dogs can get jealous. They may try and interrupt a hugging couple or bark for attention when you are on the telephone!

• • • • •

Great Dane.

Pomeranian.

Teddy Roosevelt's dog, Pete, ripped a French ambassador's pants off at the White House!

• • • • •

Obesity is the number one health problem among dogs.

• • • • •

Dogs have no sense of "time".

• • • • •

Cynophobia is the fear of dogs.

• • • • •

A person who loves dogs is called a canophilist!

• • • • •

Only dogs and humans have prostates.

• • • • •

Dachshunds were originally bred for fighting badgers.

• • • • •

Dogs judge objects first by their movement, then by their brightness, and lastly by their shape.

• • • • •

All dogs are identical in anatomy - 321 bones and 42 permanent teeth.

Irish Wolfhound.

DOGS
WORDSEARCH

R	O	L	A	Q	W	T	E	L	V	E	P
E	L	G	D	O	G	Q	P	A	T	L	S
B	T	E	S	G	X	X	L	B	E	K	D
D	A	C	H	S	U	N	D	R	R	G	F
C	N	S	F	C	P	Y	W	A	R	C	E
W	A	D	D	N	U	P	Q	D	I	D	H
V	E	N	G	K	P	I	D	O	E	N	Y
B	R	V	I	Y	P	T	S	R	R	E	P
N	V	E	J	N	Y	E	A	D	E	A	A
T	Q	W	T	X	E	S	J	S	F	D	W
E	B	A	R	K	V	A	T	G	R	W	S
S	R	B	U	C	K	E	L	P	I	E	Z

Can you find all the words below in the wordsearch puzzle on the left?

DOG   PAWS   CANINE

PUPPY   BARK   LABRADOR

DACHSUND   TERRIER   KELPIE

For more amazing facts, visit us online:

www.worldsbestfacts.com

...or follow us on Facebook:

www.facebook.com/theworldsbestfacts

Made in the USA
Middletown, DE
15 October 2017